For Fred
Rapp,
The Best

'18

A Small Pile of Feathers

A Small Pile of Feathers

The Collected Poems of Gerry Spence

by

Gerry Spence

Edited and with a Foreword
by Lori Howe

Sastrugi Press

Jackson Hole

Sastrugi Press / Published by arrangement with the author

A Small Pile of Feathers: The Collected Poems of Gerry Spence

Sastrugi Press
PO Box 1297, Jackson, WY 83001, United States
www.sastrugipress.com

Library of Congress Catalog-in-Publication Data
Library of Congress Control Number: 2017946090 (ppk) 2017946090 (hbk)
Spence, Gerry
A Small Pile of Feathers / Gerry Spence - 1st United States edition
p. cm.
1. Poetry 2. Poetry—American 3. Poetry—Places 4. Poetry—Wyoming
Summary: This collection of poetry by famous trial lawyer Gerry Spence offers a quiet moment to reflect in an otherwise noisy and chaotic world.
ISBN-13: 978-1-944986-17-9 (paperback)
ISBN-13: 978-1-944986-18-6 (hardback)
821.08'

Printed in the United States of America
Typeset with Garamond
10 9 8 7 6 5 4 3 2 1

Table of Contents

MAN IN NATURE, NATURE IN MAN

I Heard the Small Birds Sing—
Poems of Love and Family

THE WYOMING I KNOW

FOREWORD

Gerry Spence, that enduring, iconic figure in his fringed suede jacket, has been a successful, charismatic and passionate champion of justice in America's legal system for decades. Over his sixty-year career, Mr. Spence has been a guiding voice for generations of young attorneys, inspiring them to work for social justice, to remember that their own souls are key components of any true and honorable work as arbiters of law.

A prolific writer across multiple genres, as well as a professional photographer, Mr. Spence has written extensively and passionately in nonfiction books about the evolution of law, politics, and justice in America, and is a respected voice in the call to bring the heart of law practice into congruence with justice for all.

Those familiar with Mr. Spence's fiery imprecations against corruption in law and politics will recognize another side to his voice as a writer in this collection of poems, *A Small Pile of Feathers*; a spiritual, loving, and sometimes humorous side, one devoted to family and to preserving the wild places he writes of as though they were inscribed on his own bones, in his own blood:

> *My poems are as silent as firs,*
> *as towering and as still.*
> *I do not speak with gilded words*
> *that fall empty and pale*
> *as old snail shells along the trail.*
>
> *But in tender grasses along clear creeks,*
> *in the sound of meandering water over patient rocks,*
> *in the sharp, sweet smell of the early morning*
> *you will hear my songs. (p. 50)*

Mr. Spence has also depicted the soul of the American West in photography and narrative collections such as The *Lost Frontier: Images and Narratives*, and *Gerry Spence's Wyoming: The Landscape*. He has written and published memoir and fiction, including the novel, *Half-Moon and Empty Stars*. Now, Gerry Spence offers us the chance to take a walk through the nine decades of his extraordinary life in these collected poems.

A true highlight of this collection is section two, filled with poems honoring the deep and abiding love of Gerry Spence and his wife, Imaging, as well as his children, family, and lifelong friends. Entirely and authentically

Spence's, many of these poems capture the kind of raising of the ordinary to the sublime so often found in Pablo Neruda's sonnets, such as in Mr. Spence's poem, "Once the Legs of Wrens," a love poem for his wife, Imaging:

> *You came whisking like six new brooms into my life*
> *you, the child of the electric winds of love,*
> *and by the bread and milk of passion*
> *you dipped me into a sweet fathomed sea*
> *and captured me.* (p. 58)

These poems offer us, as readers, the chance to glimpse America through Mr. Spence's life, seeing it as he has, the sacred and ordinary makings of a career, a life dedicated to honoring the landscape of the West and those indomitable few who have and continue to struggle to inhabit the wild moods of the weather and lands of Wyoming, so beautiful in all its extremities, of the mountain west and high plains:

> *We trembled in the thunderstorms*
> *and laughed, we, safe behind the door.*
> *Some days were as blue as bottles,*
> *without a cloud, the cheerless shrouds*
> *of lurking death and silent desperation,*
> *dull and dreary,*
> *having fled the golden morning light.* (p. 100)

Of all the rivers that run through this book, perhaps the greatest one is the deep, quiet sense of grace, a current strong enough to remind us of what we value in our own lives, the people and things that help us find and keep our paths. As Mr. Spence says: *I sing out of a heart worn smooth.*

As a fellow poet, it has been my honor to serve as Mr. Spence's editor for *A Small Pile of Feathers.* These poems, as all good poems do, illuminate the moments of a life, in the way that the sun can drape itself across pebbles and shoes and wise old cedar trees in a kind of holy fire.

—Lori Howe, editor, author of *Cloudshade:
Poems of the High Plains,* and *Voices at Twilight*

A SMALL PILE OF FEATHERS

The wind in summer weather
sang its summer songs.
What must I do with that small pile of feathers?
(This morning it is gone.)

MAN IN NATURE, NATURE IN MAN

This is the yellow time of life
the aspens yellow in delight
willing to dance one last yellow dance
before the fall.
5-23-15

On the Capture of Young Ravens

I sit by the greenly willows
soft in their ever,
beside their raven shadows
in the black morning sky,

and hear the long night cawing,
the mother calling ever
through the moonlight lightly,
crying in the lost far gone,
the willows whimpering by.

Oh, back to the great dawn home
of soft feathered cawing,
and back to the roundness of the circled,
circling ever
in the mother crying by.

About 1965

Three Shades of Snow

I say, pedantically,
there are but three shades of snow:

> Spring crooked-up,
> Spring belly-blue,
> and robin-breasted in the mating season.

All others for the sake of reason
fell beneath a bed of roses
that springtime morning,
the red wings protesting in the rushes
and honeycombs of frenzied bees
stunned in bitter wind and freezing flake.

It was here by this pool of pollywogs
that I cried,
"If only I could sun the dankness
of these midnight innards
and dry the frigid hair inside my soul."

It was here I smelled the old stench
of winter, repudiated by wild plum buds—
bursting in their orange and mostly white shrine,
and I,
mighty,
pure and exemplified, and quick-frozen
became the softest, grey life-juices
of the oyster
and the oyster shell,
and of wee trembling mermaids
by the tall lilied snow bank of the forest.

And here I became:

       trampled by mothers,
       broken in red grasses,
       sunned in weeping willows,
       sweetened in the antlers
       of baby June-bugs,

wetted down with the manure of old joys,
dripped dry,
and fondled by rock chucks.

With nomadic fingers I loved
and wept in the leavened snow bank,
banked and beautiful
and filled with frozen fairies.
There I lay me down,
crooked-up and belly blue,
with robins in the mating season
to sing,
and die.

      About 1967

Departure from Dry Creek

We are gathered here together,
you and I,
the sassy, slapdash sky a careless blue.
We speak laconically of love
as we weep.
        (Will I grow fat on a diet of weeping?)

For I come to stack the mattresses
against the rats,
and to leave sweet-scented shooting stars
rolling violet in the springtime,
        (to whom I never thought to say goodbye).

I come to close out the summer,
to batten cabin doors
against winter blizzards,
        (the white writhings
        of wrathful winter wizards.)

In the light of sun-warmed under-grass
newly greened
from tardy rain,
I am
painful and stiff
like summer stems
that stand
dead,
and then face two inches of drizzle.
        (The withered lizards' cloaking laughs
        deep into their reptile gizzards).

And the grasshoppers snapping by,
rattling before the dead,
unable to sing quietly

with befitting reverence
for the last days of dying summer,
as if rowdy boys had tied tin grasshopper cans
to their wings.
>   (The frost will quiet them down,
>   stiffen
>   and slow,
>   and cause arthritis
>   of old grasshoppers and old men).

I'm here to throw one long, splintery kiss
to the woodpile,
piled up in a lattice of wood shadows,
the wood to my armpits,
a chipmunk's skyscraper,
and a lifesaver
when attacked by a summer's
uninvited icy fit.

And before Dry Creek (I never saw it dry)
freezes only on its surface
like a bashful girl,
but warm and wiggly,
gurgly, harmless underneath,
>   (a brook trout safe within her innards
>   below the winter wizards)
let me make a new Burpee's Catalogue of seeds:

Mountain dandelion—(common dandelion in the mountains).
I had worried that its total pasture yellows
would suffocate the younger fellows,
but now I see the brome grass' omnipresent red.
>   (As my father used to say,
>   "Every dog has his day,"
>   if that is relevant
>   to the meadow bed).

But the catalogue:
>Prairie paintbrush
>light cadmium red and lush,
>the scrubby cinquefoil,
>aged, bent, bearing yellow roses
>and north of the hand-hewed cabin,
>blue penstemon noses.

I sound like a botanist,
but I learned you by your names
because I loved you.

>Yarrow—
>yarrow—
>white achillea yarrow-
>(frozen in the white tomorrow)
>blue hair bells, and lighter blue wild iris,
>(poison on the Indian's spear).

I kiss you all.
Burpee makes a better catalogue
than I, a poem,
which does not place much honor upon Burpee.

It will be like strangling
my own tight throat
to shut down the headgate.
The water in the pasture veins will stop.
I should throw the headgate wide open,
with a hero's flourish: The speech:
>Flow forever, if you can.
>Live,
>yes, flood these hundred-forty acres
>with your crystal waters
>until the ditches have disintegrated
>and the once dead grass has faded
>and the sagebrush has returned—
>unburned.

I have known many a good friend

with good flesh and good veins
whose headgates were shut down too soon.

What a question you ask!
        "If I were immortal would I love you?"
I do not answer such questions.
Like the wise dog at my feet,
I only know my brother has visited and gone.
The young ravens have feathered and gone.
Old Indian John has come for a laugh and a nod
and a shot of good whiskey, and gone.
My children of the summer have grown and gone.
The robin from the greenly willow
and the blackbirds, singing
(noise-making, I'd say),
on the fence stay
are gone,
gathered at some apple orchard
a thousand feet below,
son and daughter, black and sleek,
I knew them when they were fuzzy yellow.
I found one, brown speckled egg
unhatched, alone.
Blown from the nest
by careless winds.
I thought I knew it.

I put the padlock on the gate
to lock out what or whom I do not know,
except five months of winter blizzards
and five feet of winter snow.
I put my tears in my pockets,
and I go.

About 1967

Fire on Table Mountain

You could hear the silence roaring,
the geese high flying,
great smoking holes burned through fear,
our leaden tears too heavy
for late summer crying.

We stood at the other side of singing,
beside vast caverns gaping, drying,
as black as burnt bluebells,
the withered eyes of blinded peaks
too parched for weeping,
too scorched for dying.

We plugged our ears
against the beating of the smoke,
with stiffened fingers
against pine needles crying,
curling
like fingers of spastic babies.
We heard the forest weeping
like lamentations of loving mothers
lingering after rosaries,
after the snow was charred,
and small, fat, furry beasts
were rendered lard.

About 1970

God of the Meadow

Comes a light mid-summer fright,
like friends dying in the night
before their time,
when daisies quit their springtime dances
with rain and sun
and fall flattened to the ground.
And yesterday's high green pasture turns dead brown.

I suppose I'm anxious
(slightly anxious)
from my memory of standing here
a few June afternoons ago—
(at least ten hot ones in a row—)
to see the dandelions and
the alsike clover, lush and luxuriant
cover everything this side of the creek
as if they were immortal,
          (without the wisdom of passing pain,
            or a history of ephemeral tears)
laughing their thunderously
silent laughs on a verdant spree
of springtime joy
like some romping, rowdy boy.

An herbage army
had invaded,
conquered,
smeared and defiled
the countryside
with one backhanded swipe
of green, as if no other pigment
lay on the planet's pallet.
And the meadowed world
blindly followed

like tumbling children
possessed by the vernal voodoo
of some adolescent guru.

Should I neglect my clear duty
to a mindless meadow in midsummer?
That is the question.
To rebuff panic at its dying
seemed quite mortal in decrying
times too early for the party's end.

And so I tread as a simple servant
to the meadow
to free a good head of water
for the pasture ditches.
I go where
Lundy Thayer, my predecessor,
fought the battle,
a hard-working, honest man
with a heart as straight
as his open, sun-burned face.

I go to dam up the headgate
with the hay down flat
and the threat of thunder.
I used to wonder,
how Lundy Thayer could spare
a single day, year after year
to fix the waterway
when he could beat
that yearly chore of plugging up the holes
with gunny sacks, and pounded mud and rock.
Yes, one could win the yearly war
with hunks of iron and chunks of concrete.

The work starts by shedding
overalls and boots,

but not the shirt.
An unequivocal decree proclaims
not to flirt with charging hordes
of mosquitoes
who await their share
and more
of hide and hair.

Then step into the waters
crystal clear and icy from the glaciers.
It must afford a spectacle
to see me standing
white-legged, with the grace
of a shuddering stork
and with the little lacy tongues
of a herd of virgin water angels
lapping at my naked fork.

I marked the water level with
a twig before I started.
I dug the rocks
off last year's bottom,
piled them up,
plugged the holes,
with who knows whose
old rotted bed sheets
and holey gunny sacks
left there last year
by Lundy Thayer.
I stuck more sticks in between the rocks,
and mudded up the leaky spots—
like Lundy Thayer, yes, beaver-like.
I shoved and patted in the sod
and watched the water level rise
two magic inches to my surprise.

It's a blessed pleasure
to be god to a meadow,
and a servant to its grasses,
an uninvited joy
that collapses time
and launches
the forgotten journey back
from man to boy.

About 1973

Love as Flying Tulips

I saw love as flying tulips
immersed in the touch-place of spring.
They exploded
in the wake of buzzards' wings
and spewed red petals behind the sun.

I saw this from afar,
understood it under waxen feathers,
grasped the naked shroud
like dogs at the seminary
barking new tunes.
And I laughed,
because laughter has no meaning in the joke.

Cry out, oh, villain!
Beg the heat of summer
with tears of rain,
the summer of your air-conditioned fantasy.
You who seek eternity have it
in the dusty leavings of old men
and the leafy dew of giggling children.

There are no saddles for waves,
no rudders or courses for impetuous stars,
no grapes for the wine of eternity
or songs sung from the lips of the dead.
And we rejoice in the choir of sparrows.
"Goodbye," I said,
but the words rippled in the stream,
and were forgotten in the high notes of tomorrow.

A Few Leaves Fall from the Trees

A few leaves fell from the trees
while the rest stayed green and rustling
without pain.
I have not asked why.
A few leaves on the trees
turn yellow and fall
while the rest laugh in the rain.
I have not asked why.

8-31-08

On A Young Osprey Leaving the Nest

At the last, blithe breath of summer,
the blood-billed father flew the nest,
the hungry sisters and brothers, too.
But mothers?
Mothers do not fly,
not when the last
of her hatch
of the fish hawk chicks
hangs on,
whimpering, crying
in pleading squawks
known only to those
fluent in fish hawk talk.

Each day as I passed that pile of sticks
I hoped the last of the hatchlings
had, with all the rest,
fled the empty nest.
But there he sat,
like a boisterous, brazen brat
      squacking,
       talking
in baby fish hawk talk.

Sometimes he cried down at me
as if I bore some duty
to this unadopted child,
as if my hearing
his sad pubescent screeches
would end his endless
      crying
       as if in dying.

Then the aspen leaves turned yellow
and this fellow, fully feathered
in high, blood-borne bloom,
but with no intent of giving up
his room and board,
sat squawking, balking
at the call of freedom, and still
          peering,
          jeering
at the smell of threatening winter
that gave the icy rivers shivers.

Then on the first clear day of winter
he finally flew the nest,
joined his sisters and his brothers,
granted freedom to his mother,
and with little choice
but to face the strife
of becoming a grown-up fish hawk,
he ceased his endless, helpless beseeching,
screeched no more,
and flew to where life swims easy in the rivers,
where mothers, brothers and blood-billed fathers
along with full-feathered sisters
find fine, fresh fish for daily feasting.

2013

The Raven Came

The raven came,
looked in my window
and in disgust
quickly left,
as if to say,
"Surely you know
I'm not a seed-eater.
Besides,
how much notice do you need?
How much more needless cawing
to greet me
with a piece of meat?"

Winter 2014

Robert Frost Got Lost

Always liked his old broken voice.
Sounded like a frog with laryngitis.
Liked the stories of his verses.
And more than once
I've stopped by woods
on a snowy evening,
and, of two roads that diverged
in a yellow stand,
I, too, have taken the road less traveled.

Some say he's fallen out of style,
but his verse diverged across two centuries.
Some say he was a grouchy old man,
but there's part of him in me that I protect
like good secrets.

Someday I'd like to return,
and meet him along a country road,
and, as two young imperious singers,
become wild swingers of birches.

    6-12-14

Walk in the Night

I stole life from the innocent air
and breathed joy from obliging rocks.
I fell into the sheltered blanket of the night,
covered in folds of bright delight.
My bare feet caressed the gentle ground,
and in silken moonlight
I heard the forsaken sounds
of distant loons.

July 2015

Caretaker of Young Aspens

The snow fell last night on young aspens
and bent their branches.
Then you came along
and, carefully,
shook them free.
I did not see you.

　　　　For Bob Weil, Editor,
　　　　W.W. Norton and Company

Remembering Robert R. Rose, Jr.

Here I sat with you,
still,
wordless,
the lightless night
weary, retreating with shame
from the searing sun
in smokeless flame.

Here I sat with you,
your eyes gouged out
by the careless fingers of time.

Blind,
you charged into the light,
wrestled with the divine,
and having won,
danced on
into the night.

Here I sat with you
by this cedar, this gnarly saint,
it and you the same.
Ah, storm and rain,
ah, beat of sun,
ah, blessed mirth,
ah, enduring years,
and pain of birth,
ah, snows of struggle,
to and from the earth.

On the Winter Side of Man

Could we once more be like playful children—
could we dance and sing and even love
and end our wars of avarice and wrath?
If our wretched world could grasp the grace of peace
and, like babies, turn our silken cheeks
to friendly fires in mothers' sight,
the warmest place in winter's night.
        But no.
        Still no.
For we were born to scorn
the ecstasy of love's warm light
and embrace the darkness of the eternal night,
        the dark, eternal night,
        the deep, too-dark eternal night.
We were born on the winter side of man,
and sworn to live our piteous time
through blood and thorn.
While mothers suckle infants
who grow to killers,
        baby killers,
        brave, baby killers,
bound by ignorant promises to fathers
        and to their ignorant killer-fathers
        and to their worshiped, ignorant killer-fathers
        of killer-fathers
to detest and murder babies
in the shelter of their mothers' nests.

May 6, 2015

Joy Became a Treacherous Stranger

They come circling, circling,
the wary water waiting,
waiting,
the summer's loon long gone,
the old goose in the lead
her peaked eyes piercing,
piercing
the treacherous shores,
the gawking children following
in a wedge-shaped platoon,
black beaks on black tails,
old ghosts of fatal pasts
in cattail reeds leering,
leering.

Still marking the later summer air
with their circling,
circling,
twenty sets of eyes peering,
peering,
the morning moon slipping
into fog,
the wings of geese waving,
waving
like happy children
to inviting, restful waters.

The sun shines on shore rocks,
the mirrored water beckoning,
the wings of geese setting,
setting.
Then like a shot in the frozen night
the coyote springs from his lair
and by a coyote's hair

misses the lead goose flaring,
flaring.

And I pray small prayers.
Come back.
Come back.
Oh, frightened flock
light on my soul.
It will enfold you with delight.

How could they know
they need not flee from me?
When I stood, my shadow struck the coyote
and he fled.
And in that dark bed of danger
joy became a treacherous stranger.

Mountain Climbers

Some hid their poetry in the back pages of the Holy Bible
because they knew that any who survived them
would never read either.

They all wrote poetry,
those misfits caught in eternal adolescence,
those naive mountain monks
who believed in the goodness of man
without knowing why,

and who saw life as valuable
in non-saleable ways
and earthly goods as irrelevant
unless, of course, they could get you across the space
of a sheer rock face.

His kind believed that experience was it,
not some predacious goal sought in panic,
not personal power that sputters
until it's refueled with the blood of men and babies,
not money—certainly not numb, dumb money.
Life was a free fall through a hole without boundaries
that celebrated the quality of anguish one felt,
the style in which one bore pain,
with or without tears,
the grace with which one experienced joy,
deeply and silently in the fall
or by letting it fly in great yodels across a canyon wall.

These climbers of mountains believed in a natural justice,
in karma, whatever that was supposed to be.
Few ever experienced justice,
natural or otherwise
in the high, lean air where ravens go to die.

Yet they never surrendered.
No. Not yet.

They wrote more poems.
Better that they shine their boots,
or post want ads for muted mates,
or jump up and down
on half rotted stumps
to declare the coming of Jesus.

They wrote about the mystery:
of what, they never said,
and the meaning of which
they never suggested.
They wrote about nameless streams
that descended from the high meadows
like gleaming threads of silver,
about the teeth marks of beavers in old tree stumps
and the wetness of grass after quick showers,
and the desperate darkness of endless miles of deadfalls.
They wrote of hiding from a marauding mother moose,
and of avalanches that had taken out a friend
like a fly smothered in spilled soup.

They wrote of lost loves, because their women raged,
and their women begged,
and their women wept,
and their women always left them.
And they wrote of despair,
of hanging on in lonely nights,
and they also wrote of fires in the hearth against their chilling ribs,
and the sounds in the room that were silent sounds.
Yet they never surrendered.
No. Not yet.

These climbers of mountains built their lives on faith
that it would all work out,

that they would at least be loved,
at least accepted,
at least not hated,
at least not attacked and maimed.
At least not killed.
And some were maimed
and some were killed
and some nearly starved to death as they gladly,
even fervently sacrificed their youth
to perfect a difficult move on an overhanging cliff
a thousand feet above the ground,
or only five feet above the ground,
it made no difference, for no one saw their triumphs.

They rarely spoke of their successes
and, in return, they asked
that no judgments be leveled against them,
at least no colorless criticism,
at least that no charges be filed,
at least no convictions returned,
at least not banishment
nor demand for surrender—
well then, at least no order to deliver up their souls
in retribution for their crimes,
for their refusal to join the swarming, screaming masses
hugging gray concrete with tinted glasses,
in retribution for their irreverent repudiation
of the smart-ass money men
clutching to profits and climbing, climbing,
climbing over great mountains of the dead
and the near dead,
over flailing, sweating, white, soft, surrendered retching bodies,
climbing,
climbing to the cadence of hollow screams
echoing across the concrete canyons
to the summit of a colorless nothing
where the view is a wasteland of broken bottles of the soul
and empty cans of dreams,

and pigeons peck at the sidewalks
talking in pigeon talk
hoping for a roaming, vagrant ant.

The likes of the nameless climbed the rock faces.
They claimed they climbed something solid,
something connected to the stars.
But they were the cursed Sisyphus
sentenced to up-climb and down-climb
forever.
And even in the hereafter their footprints
would be slogged into the mountainsides of Mars,
and thereafter all the Jupiters in the universe,
not to mention an eternal singeing of the feathers on their angel wings
as they climb too closely to the sun.
So be it.
But the mountains they climbed were composed mostly of themselves.
Yet they never surrendered.
No. Not yet.

And then to fill their bellies that grew lean and shrunken
and accustomed to the regularity of irregular feeding, they compromised,
as we all must compromise,
and they became mountain guides
two-and-a-half months a year,
and joined the search and rescue teams
for which they received shameful pittances.
These men who took the lives of the rich and the famous into their hands
and the whiney, pale-livered sons of the rich,
were paid less than babysitters,
less than the eager-faced kids at McDonald's,
and they lived in small huts and scraped by.
When they got sick no one called the doctor,
and when their mothers died, they did not send flowers.
They sent a small note that read, "I know you now understand, Mom."
And they called on certain mysterious forces for replenishment,
and they felt the perverse joy of not having surrendered.
No. Not yet.

Death of the Pine Siskin

My tears appeared,
welling up from under lids.
Tears love the living
and never wet the eyes of the dead.

On my deck the wind danced with a dead bird
half the size of a sparrow,
and gave life to the lifeless little fellow.
The rollicking wind blew with beat and song
swinging the wind's tiny feathered partner
so in the wind's dancing with the dead
the bird's ivory breast was bared,
a brave yellow bar across it quiet wings,
its legs and feet, no larger than pencil marks,
pointed to the careless sky.

Then to display its mate of late
the wind whirled up its partner's cocoa-colored back,
then its creamy breast again.
And, without knowing,
the injudicious wind
by its immaculate blowing
delivered life and heart to the departed.

I expected the feathers
to pull themselves together
and fly away.
All the while other birds
went hip-hopping by,
inspecting the piles of seeds I'd left for them.
They paid no heed to their fallen brother.
For them the law of death feeds no meaning
nor an empty craw.

7-14-15

Water

Find the seeping spring,
you'll find the settler's cabin.
Find the high clear streams,
you'll find the beaver's dam,
where herds of deer
drink behind the grizzly,
and where all that covet life,
the mountain ram,
the prairie hen,
will soon appear
for water.

Find the rivers
and you'll find
the dreams of man
whose hand
turned vacant prairies
into fields of hay
with water on the land.

Hear the gentle rush of water
falling, tumbling down
the mountain sides,
like the sounds of mother
softly singing to the child.
See the waters of the sea,
its salt the precursor of sweat,
the stuff of tears
that stain the passage
of the years,
its covering depths where
life began,
and most of the living

on this tortured earth reside
and hide from hungry,
careless, killing man.

These clear mountain waters,
the universe of trout,
where men
relinquish their money-grabbing carnage
for a day to play once more as boys,
their bellies light
their minds delight
casting an inviting fly
in peaceful waters
to catch a fry.

But remember…
men will slaughter
son and daughter
saint or neighbor
with gun or saber
when at stake
for dominion's sake
is but one drop of water.

The Tetons

In times long fled, while fancy men
and frilly women
paraded on the condescending streets of Paris,
here, in far Wyoming,
in this wild and treacherous land,
savage outcasts with knives
and traps of steel in hand
fought vicious storms
and incarcerating ice and death
in search of wealth from bloody hides of beaver,
their fur forfeited to forge high top hats
for the swaggering French
under silken dress
and natty spats in high top fashion.

With the passion
and the fervor of the famished
those lusty, lonely trappers,
discarded by the flock
but with ruddy health
and unrequited dreams of wealth,
and of the soft, moist touch of naked breasts
named these imperious protrusions
into the heights of sightless skies,
these towering peaks, "The Tetons."

These haughty, heady peaks
rising from the common
without embarrassment,
that greet the bitter wind and freezing sleet
with unfathomable elation—
hot heads in summer frost,
bare heads lost in blinding blizzards,
their singing voices heard

by chirping marmots in the rocks
by flocks of listening birds,
and injudicious climbers
against their granite shocks.

These peaks
speak to us, the panicked species,
our mouths agape,
that we, too, might escape
the common plain where most have trod
plodding, nodding,
like a herd of spineless sycophants,
like an endless line of tired, compliant, marching ants.

These pompous peaks have stood
against the violent terrors of the storm—
the strikes of lightning from all sides
against their naked, rocky, ruptured hides,
these patient peaks
like suffering parents endure the noise
of their rowdy, adolescent boys.

These despotic peaks
that penetrate a virgin sky
mock my courage.
I squint like the faint, beholden
with worship in surrendered eyes.
I stand humbled in their shadows
and digest as the feast of day
my loathsome fear of their majestic stand
in this feral, hallowed land.

But before I meekly slip
into the waiting mist of nothingness,
head bent in shameless sufferance,
let me just once
stand straight

and bravely seek
the lofty top
of my uncharted,
disregarded—
my patiently awaiting,
undiscovered heights.

Summer Solstice

The thunder snarled, burbled, bellowed
and made all nature of threatening noise
to scare the children.

I thought it an inconvenient thing to do,
worse, inconsiderate
considering that the bam and rumble
frightened small birds as well.

Then came eleven minutes of hard rain
that suddenly ended like an old man coughing
his last cough
before the onset of the noisy silence.

"It is over," I heard a mute voice holler.
"I told you this was just a passing blip
in the slumber of the Blue Sky."

Territorial Imperative

(a true story)
They call it the "territorial imperative"
of man and chirping bird,
a word for fearless frogs and pollywogs,
and all other creatures who struggle
to preserve their right to place
against those who'd drive them
from their consecrated space.

Among the sons of robins,
it's singing their invading neighbors
out of the neighborhood.
It should,
at 4:00 o'clock
of a summer's morning.

But I had, instead, become
captured by the territorial imperative of the dead.
Their kin were insisting
that the old cedar tree
at the Crystal Springs Cemetery must go.
"Yes, it must go," the family said,
who spoke with humbled reverence
through their emissary,
our dear Aunt Flo—
keeper of the grounds,
preserver of the wall,
protector of us all,
(God bless her thrifty, southern,
all-American, practical,
economical, and utilitarian soul.)

As I have said,
the dead

were demanding certain rights,
and Aunt Flo,
also their representative
in Mississippi agreed:
When all things were considered
thoroughly,
and in the best of light,
including the territorial rights
of headstones,
of crumpled caskets—
(those rotted baskets of old bones)—
the tree must go.

That tree was pushing down the family wall,
"Something there is that doesn't love a wall,"
the poet laureate once decreed
but not speaking of the buried dead.
Still, as far as I could see,
that stubborn root-entangled tree,
could survive us all,
all,
except our dear Aunt Flo.

"That tree must go," she said again.
"It's invaded our sacred territory.
There's no room for one more of us.
It's taken over our space
to be,
and to un-be,
to which I cannot,
will not,
no, will never once agree."

I said, "I agree not to spare that tree.
One is entitled to claim one's place,
to cut off the tired edge of life,
and to descend, heavily, into the soundless,
timeless, ground.

And how may we, we pray,
terminate this monotony of strife
and stripped life,
if there's no room left to lie down
in the Crystal Springs Cemetery?
Tell me that."

And so the heirs sharpened their wits
and shared their collective advice.
Some were for axe,
some for tree poison,
and some thought an action in
a court of law
for the tort
of the cedar tree's trespass would be right—
or a careful sawing in the night.

But later, on the brink of dreaming,
I found myself thinking
it would be good
to snuggle, belly-down,
beneath the old tree's roots
and to pop out
some bright blue Mississippi morning
as a cedar berry—
a cherry for the hungry birds.

And despite our dear Aunt Flo
I thought the territory of the tree
should be authenticated, adjudicated,
recorded, exemplified, certified, and decreed
for all to know that that old cedar tree
was free to grow
and grow,
and to be
along its uninterrupted path to eternity—
and so I argued to our dear Aunt Flo.

Days later I was downright astounded
when Aunt Flo,
who is traditionally grounded
in predictably practical and dispassionate positions,
bent to my argument.
"Perhaps it is more fitting," she said
"that we respect the living over the dead,
and that includes the tree."
The rest of the heirs were too timorous,
too drearily docile to take offense,
and to avoid an out-and-out collision
with Aunt Flo's decision
without the first derision
they all caved.
And, thereby, that grand old tree was saved.

Then one day I got a wire
From Aunt Flo who reported
that the cedar tree had just expired.
What?
How could this be?
But she was quick to explain:
Without invitation
or expectation,
a twister had made its unsolicited visit
to the Crystal Springs Cemetery.

And it chose one place to touch down—
the ground that held that plaguing old tree.
Around and around the twister spun
in her impish, irresponsible, whirling fun.
She had decided to dance with that old tree.
And when the music stopped
she dropped it,
roots and all
on the other side of the standing wall.

First Snow

Together we watched the snow cover the ground
in ten minutes.
"Before it's through
the snow will be up to the doorknob."
Do you remember saying that?

Then we saw the golden ground give up,
the tall summer grasses, frightened,
standing stiff
like old men frozen at the brink
waiting to be smothered.

"Do not be afraid, grasses," you said.
"Already you have seeded.
Do not shiver so.
But fight." Do you remember how you said,
"Oh, please fight!"
And then the blood of golden grasses
turned all white.

Fare for Kings

Blessed mothers fight the plight
of bitter winter storms
that threaten half-starved children,
the snow, roof high,
      yet higher still,
      yet higher still,
bewildering piles of white upon the land
dumped by soundless, mindless hands
diminishing towering spruce and lofty peak
while last year's surrendered grasses
      fall fast asleep,
      fast asleep.
And across the whitened weary vale
pale coyote mothers yelp
at gawking moons
and half-lit stars,
and often fail to score
some careless rabbit
with the fatal habit
of wandering from its frozen door.
While in the coyote's hungry den
five furry, feral pups
whine and whimper,
      searching here,
      searching there,
for any morsel, any meat
to at last retreat from under
the pangs of gnawing hunger.

The forest hen, the winter wren,
their hatches fled
to warmer climes
sing mother-songs to empty winter air,
ever watching carefully,

carefully here,
    carefully there,
set for sudden flight from hungry hawks
that stalk such birds
for winter's sparse delight.

And I sit warmly by the fire
and take the offered fare of kings,
immune from that insidious fight
for the simple right to eat,
as if my right to live were bestowed
on me at birth in contradiction of the worth
of winter's other creatures on the planet Earth.

Ah, the Early Light

Ah, the early light is the light—
nets of light,
lattices of light,
great glowing tubs of light
spilled by careless hands
on quivering aspens
and jagged peaks
made molten at their edges.

In the early light the air
snaps at the ears
so straight, so shrill
old boulders crack.
The magpie squawks.
The marmot chirps.
The coyote whines,
begging the sun to warm
his shedding fur, his bony spine.
At last he slumbers in the early light
as silent and smiling
as budding buttercups.

In the early light the breath of horses
creates yellow mist,
nose hairs kissed with frost,
jaws smashing golden grasses
and brave, white prairie daisies,
lost in nature's imposed strife
of life for life.

And once, in the early light,
A great bull elk, its rack in velvet,
walked among the horses,
trampled over pink wild geraniums,
and disappeared into a purple web of shadows.

To the Killers

You would kill the whole Earth,
and poison its seas
with ceaseless disease
for a day's quick profit,
you sick, insane killers,
you distillers of death.

You kill the trees
you obdurate fools,
you mindless collections of cells,
your stuffed eyes locked to the bottom line,
you who have not walked one step
through the parched tears
of rotting jungles
or scabbed-over prairies,
your fat asses
welded to your boardroom chairs.

You morticians from hell
saw the legs from the forests,
sell their splintered corpses,
smash its flowers into dust.
You impotent yowlers,
who cannot create a worm,
when you have finished singing
the profit songs of idiots
and of paper dollar ghouls
and lie down to die
the earth will digest you
with love.

I HEARD THE SMALL BIRDS SING—

POEMS OF LOVE

AND FAMILY

From desperate jungles, quarter to empty,
late in the afternoon the sun broke through.
You came up the same dark trail.

Small drops glistened on your forehead,
your eyes, intense like the small yellow bird's
in the old oak tree.

We sang the wordless, voiceless song
and danced our stepless dances,
lost gypsies in the twilight
to the silent beat of great gray wings.
To Imaging on Valentine's Day, 2008

No Words

No words, no yellow roses,
no thunder at the windowsill,
no song from some mad troubadour at the door,
no crazy frolicking in new green prairie grasses,
no walking backwards in the snow,
no clandestine meeting in crumbling hotels,
the light, a single bulb, hanging from the ceiling,
the flag flapping,
clapping at the sight of lovers,
a calendar of Jesus on the wall.

No flying in circles back to one another
like one-winged birds,
no feral music of the heart,
the songs of geese, joined in mating song for life,
and, despite the danger of the hunters' guns,
no crying out their wild, unfettered joy,
no free laughter of children running in the prairie wind,
chasing dreams not yet stricken from the mold,
no shoes that in the morning are revisited
by feet that touched you in the night,
no home without candles of inviting light,
no wild, winter birds who give birth
to courageous songs,
no words that tell
of our lives together
that escape the boundless language of the earth.

For Imaging, remembering those beginnings.

I Speak Only of Mercury and Mars

Sun,
yes, you out there,
you, silent sun.
Listen!
I speak only of Mercury and Mars
inside the kettle drum, the sounds of life,
the heart,
(the irreprehensible beating
of the heart).

I have heard the great speeches,
made them with the noise of prophets,
I have aimed young eyes at heaven
and dredged the dreaded harbors of life,
explored their murky waters,
and then touched bluebells gently in the spring.
And I have seen them shy
like young owlets dropped into the sky
too early.

Please do not shiver one more time
or turn a frozen shoulder to the wind.
Do not retreat to rock.
I cannot embrace the mountainside.
I am a poor wizard
alone with my minor magic.
And you,
you of the sun,
and of Mercury and Mars,
you, who beat into the empty spaces
of my kettle drum,

you will not pass like mist on Buck Mountain
nor summer's snow on great peaks,
nor like the tears of bluebells.
You dare not.
You dare not.

To Imaging on Christmas, 1986

I Walked Through the Forest

I walked through the forest,
saw it burst in bright, forgiving blossoms of summer,
saw it bend under the laden pink of wild geraniums,
saw it struggle against the boast of blue lupine,
and gently writhe from the pain of its own glory.

And the forest, silent as sleeping stars,
shouted my verses, whispered in your ear,
and embraced you with hungry arms
beside the fecund fern,
the hair bell, blue as early skies,
the curious crocus climbing its fragile shadows
to grasp a glimpse of its gentle passing.

I do not wail.
I do not exclaim from mountain tops.
My tears are veiled like frightened fawns.
I do not sing sweet sylvan songs
nor shout balmy springtime sonnets.
My poems are as silent as firs,
as towering and as still.
I do not speak with gilded words
that fall empty and pale
as old snail shells along the trail.

But in tender grasses along clear creeks,
in the sound of meandering water over patient rocks,
in the sharp, sweet smell of the early morning,
you will hear my songs.

For Imaging, Christmas, 2000

Old Love

Something about old love does not wither
like daisies at the end of summer.
White petals brown and curling,
their tender lust forgotten in the rush.
But old love is not like that.

I sing out of a heart worn smooth,
the creek rocks also smooth,
the waters wear,
not in anger or despair,
time calling like the rippling sun
begun at noon and left alone to pout.
But old love is not like that.

My love for you is old, worn lovely,
worn beyond the heat at noon
beyond the hungry standing tassels
beyond the puff and tilt
of men and birds evaporated
into smokeless skies,
my love for you arises like young tulips
from old ground into your gathering eyes.

To Imaging on Valentine's Day, 2000

I Should Sing Wild, Hungry Songs

I should sing wild, hungry songs
that disrobe the cloaking night,
that set the forest quivering,
and small haired and hairless beasts
with eyes like bulging black marbles
scurrying in sudden frightened flight.

I see them,
tightened bellies to the ground,
ears like rising muffins in the pan,
bulging, straining at the sound,
slick, wet noses searching,
tingling in their reaching,
timid against the thunder's blast
in the passing showers of the night.

I see them,
transmogrified into whispers of old leaves
skittering to the forest floor,
like careless children wandering to the door.
I see small, soft, silken creatures, blinking
against the blinding of their passing shadows,
against long, half-staring moons,
the forest staggered and stilled,
stunned that such unrequited power
can be renewed
in a single, trembling drop of dew.

Suddenly the forest thrush dares sing.
Yes, I say,
such is the sound escaping
from my being.
Suddenly the bashful sky reopens,
blue arms reaching.

Yes, I say,
such are my arms for you,
beside a fallen leaf,
beneath a drop of dew.

For Imaging, Christmas, 2000

Silence Sang Its Eulogy

They had crept out of their graves,
those stony conceptions on the crest,
like awakening mothers looking down,
the sun warming their pregnant, granite bellies,
among the stiff and blackened dead,
their charred limbs lifted,
beseeching,
singing a silent requiem.
It was here I brought you with the weeping
during flashes of sight from the dead, stony blind,
you, that one small bucket of gray cold ashes.

I struggled up the mountainside of memories
where the sting of being
was transformed to your singing
(outrageously out of tune)
with our mother still on note,
and my sack of childish wisdom
filled with certainty that such songs
would always be (whatever "forever" meant)
along with you, our old Model A
and good fishing every Sunday.

I did not weep—
the silent ring of your assurance
on that delightful fall day,
that death was life's reward
of eternal sleep.
         Eternal sleep.

I spoke to the bucket.
"Speak to me, dear father."
I waited.
All I heard was the spiking of a distant bird

against the withering peak.
I asked again,
and silence sang its eulogy.

Then I lifted you in my hands,
as once you lifted me when I had fallen.
And now you've passed once more,
beyond my sight, beyond my searching eyes
as blind as those lifeless granite heights.

I asked for just one word,
and you left me wordless as the blackened trees
burned, stiffened and bleak
as me, your first begotten, also stiffened
by a nod of thoughtless years.

Oh, father, you who have escaped your ashes,
you, the creator of budding springtime memories
in this grieving fall,
I breathe you in,
absorb the dust of your bones
like the early morning mist
and exhale you into the careless wind.

I see you mixing up the pancake batter
of a Sunday morning,
now, the living leavened with the ashes of the dead.
I, your tearless son, hover at the brink
of that yawning precipice,
saddened, and rejoicing, and already old.
Then I said, "I wish to be your child again."

Mae, Dad's beloved wife, was with him at the moment of his passing.
She reported his last words, as follows:

"Honey, it's time for me to go, but I don't want to leave you alone."

Mae said, "'Honey, you can go.' And she told me, "He smiled at me, closed his eyes and he was gone."

Both he and Mae said it was their wish that their ashes be mixed together and spread on Green Ridge behind the farm where John and Alice Spence, our grandparents, had reared their family—Roland Spence, the eldest, a cowboy all his life (and grandpa insisted he was probably the smartest), our father, Gerald Milner Spence, a chemical engineer, and Hunter Spence, a teacher who returned to the farm for the rest of his and our grandparents' lives.

Accordingly, on Mae's death, Tom Spence, my brother, and I mixed their ashes and ascended Green Ridge on October 9, 2002, where we scattered their ashes into the prevailing wind. I have clear, fond memories of my father's unwavering bravery, his steadfast goodness, his ready wit, and his quiet, assuring voice of reason—all of which I have struggled to emulate.

Once the Legs of Wrens

Once the legs of wrens
were as large around
as century-old oaks
and forty feet to heaven,
and the cry of the turtledove
deafened ancient ears
and caused the continents
to fracture like icing
on sun-baked cakes.

Once the footprints of love left puddles
from purple rains so thick
that the sun, embarrassed,
hid for ten thousand years in the womb
of wine-sodden clouds.
Then the humming of growing grasses
sounded like shouting choir boys
and the smell of roses was so thick
that chipmunks, then the size of elephants,
staggered in the sweet syrup of delirium.

During those times of beet-red sunrises
you were born the star of Desire.
Who knows your celestial sire,
a blue-eyed black leopard in the night,
so mighty the galaxies rocked,
so rapturous the stars turned shy.

And what blessed mother do we blame?
Only the god of timeless seas
who bounced Hercules on her knees
even knows her name.
But you—you suckled at her breasts,
drank the milk of galaxies,

absorbed the high flamed wisdom
of eternal mothers, molten and silent,
as indolent as the lazy eight of infinity.
She taught you the bounteous songs of angels,
and implanted the velvet heart of saints.
She stole the candied beauty of the afterworld
promised to the last child of seven kings
and molded it on your immortal face.

Then she released you, this mother of mothers,
released you on the wings of giant larks into a downy wind,
you, destined to grace this lonely world of mine
where the legs of sparrows are but toothpicks
and the moon is frightened in the afternoon.
You came whisking like six new brooms into my life,
you, the child of the electric winds of love,
and by the bread and milk of passion
you dipped me into a sweet fathomed sea
and captured me.

And like the golden cocoon to the butterfly,
you floated into this world of cherished mothers,
you, you pagan seed, you naked egg,
you, you coral light from the eyes of stars,
you, you light-born mother of virgin forests,
you, you song-born mother of brave men,
you, your breath born of lilies
and captured in the magical web of adoring spiders,
by these timid words you shall be inhaled
into the lungs of weary, wordy history
until the blood red beaches turn to pearls
and the sons of men
drown in the oceans of your love.

To Imaging on Mother's Day, May 12, 2002

Ode to My Hero

I've known of many heroes,
ones with gaudy medals flashing in the sun,
handsome faces on the screen,
glamorous men who nodded in feigned humility,
who, garbed in all their power,
were fearful of their own tears
and terrorized of love.

You were stabbed deeply by the killing knife
of that mindless, descending malady.
And you stabbed back with your only weapon—
your clear, warbled love song for your family.
While, in my own incandescent world,
I would have quaked in unrelenting fear,
and been shrouded
in the desperate darkness of despair.

You are my hero,
you who have lived so brightly
in the shadows,
and laughed
into the ugly mask of pain
and offered peace in the face
of the terrible war you fought.
It is you who comfort me
with your brave smile
when you are the one
who has earned a universe of comforting.

I have longed for a hero—
spent a lifetime searching for one—
someone serenely brave
whose course in life
has been less stained than mine
by the merciless fear of strife.

Oh, yes, you small lady,
you are my hero.
You were able to cry when you were afraid
to feel lonely when the shadows darkened,
to wonder without fear
at the great out-there,
and at last, in peace,
to face the boundaries of life.

Remembering Marie Potash, who fought with grace and bravery and was cheerful, loving and giving to the end on June 9, 2002.

After a Third of a Century

Like the fingers of children
in the frosting,
the shuddering aspens
bear new, wet snows.
My love for you is like that
in the forest of our days.

And now after a third of a century
our roots deep and safe
in the soil of our making,
in the mulch of old love and old times,
the rich earth tumbled at our feet,
the sound of grandchildren's laughter,
our children beginning to gray,
my own thatch faded long ago
(the time of yours to be announced.)
Despite the extravagance of our love,
in these withering years
when the stony mountains of tomorrow
stand cold and reaching,
I touch you gently with a finger
(I could not shout it better on the loft of lungs)
and, whisper nothing,
blessed with your gifts
and rendered voiceless by their grandeur.

To Imaging on our 33rd anniversary

The Greatest Battle

Fourteen brave swordsman entrapped you.
I fought them all, I, the hero of Singing Trees,
I, the fair young knight who fought for you,
slew them all, three at a time at times
so great was my passion,
my love that armored my soul
with the power of a hundred charging lions.

Then I took on the evil king himself.
We fought for twenty-seven days,
and through as many nights,
bleeding into the thirsty ground
where pure white daisies bloomed,
fed by the blood of our battle.
After the king died, his heart severed
with the final thrust of my sword,
came terrible storms, and the earth parted
and I grasped the sides of the cliffs
torn from the globe by thunder
and great floods were poured over me
and I fought the torrents
until one day I awoke in your arms,
and I said, "Will you be my valentine?"
and you said, "Did you bring a box of See's Chocolates?"

For Imaging
Valentine's Day, 2004

The Coyote and the Swan

You mothers, you suffering angels,
your backs bent toiling in the yellow morning
where but the bravest angels sing,
and the breath of spring is lost
to frost threatening,
against the heavy sting of heart
for swaddling infants
too soon departed,
the too cruel cost of motherhood.

In the world of hatchling swans—
cygnets, as they're called—
those pure white, peeping, fuzzy balls—
the coyote comes slinking, skulking,
a slayer cast from hell
who lies hidden where mothers
and their babies dwell.

There, in defense of chick and child,
the wings of swans
and the enfolding arms of mothers
are broken to repel the killer's calculated catch
of mothers' helpless hatchings.

We, on our begotten plain,
fight against the pain of womb,
against our forgotten first cry
into the night
and the last—
the silent shutting of the tomb.
We seek out spaces at the feet of fools
in mad, mendacious places
of fancy suits and gaudy ties
and endless sets of lying eyes.

But the songs that sing us into night
are from the mouths of mothers.
They cling to love above the flames,
when all that then remains of swan or mother
are bloody, broken wings
hurled against the coyote at that bleeding place
where mothers face unfettered greed and hate
and strive to save us with an angel's loving grace.

To Imaging on Mother's Day, May 8, 2005

I Am Waiting for the Children

I am waiting for the children
to come rolling, hopping, chirping down,
merciless in perfect joy to attack the snow
that smothers land and landscape.

How can the children sleep
in wide-eyed times like these
when porch snow smothers
sash and sill,
where pines and pine devils
sing their pure white songs
and frozen sparrows, white as day,
laugh in frozen feathers?

                    For my grandchildren, Senia and U
                    on Christmas Day, 08

None Have Known Love but We

Many sing of love that hides like hoarded riches,
that laughs into wanton, yearning faces
and disappears in shrouded places.
None on Earth have known love but we.
All the rest are struggling strangers in different boats
sailing different, distant, petulant seas.

You have given my shuttered eyes new sight.
You have given me new fingers that touch
the beauty of the fragile light.
You have given me room to live,
and permission to die,
but only when life has faded like old newspapers.
And when we say goodbye,
we will laugh together.

And what of this year
that bursts upon us like a blind, charging bull?
Each day worth a hundred past.
I see your beauty seeping from the soul
as bright as early sun that fades the night.
But tell me, dear woman of divine delight,
how is it that you have no golden wings
in this paradise of which I sing?

To Imaging on our Fortieth
November 18, 2009

The Frozen Vales of Nowhere

Had I not been fortune's chosen,
I should have never found you hidden
in the frozen vales of nowhere.
And each day with the passion
of a thousand loving witches,
with your magic thread and thrifty stitches,
you saved me from the bottom of myself.

I predict great joy together.
In this I will not be wrong—
no, not under the lilies at the lily pond,
no, not atop the peaks of mulish mountains,
no, not under beds of silky sheets or flossy feathers,
no, not in the ascending songs of fire,
no, not at the blessed bright beginning,
nor the eternal ending of the ethereal choir.

To Imaging, date unknown.

An Ode to the King

We were lost in bitter, entangled jungles,
crying to emptied ears.
We were tormented by a blank-eyed,
merciless fate who chortled at our pain.
So we beseeched the king.

Some kings are as wise as moldy stumps,
some foolish as young magpies in springtime.
But yours was a benevolent kingdom,
your crown an intractable love.
You heard us with ears of the saint,
and like the paint of old masters
you spread your riches in kind and kindness
on the canvas of our lives.

The last I saw you I reached for your hand,
and I said, "There are no goodbyes.
I will see you tomorrow."
And, oh dear King, we have always
spoken the truth to each other.

Remembering Alan Hirchfield, 1-24-15

I Heard the Small Birds Sing

I heard the small birds sing,
their voices seeping through the walls of heaven.
I bathed in warm, departed waters,
that soothe the raw, seared flesh of being.

I saw the splendor
of boasting mountains ringing,
slashing through eternal skies,
and tireless oceans that rise and float
the weary continents of the globe.

I tasted the lavish works
that ravish the fecund funds
of famous chefs,
and smelled the smothered scent of roses
in the royal gardens, begging for unsullied air.

I felt the wanton softness of royal, silken sheets
and touched the soft sweet cheeks of babies
moist from their mothers' breath.

But you, oh, you are the creator
of living paradises.
You mock the march of death.
You invite the entanglement of my soul,
the reaching fingers of my tormented heart,
the trembling mountains of my strength,
the timid tenderness that embraces my feral flaws
with love.

     To Imaging on her Sixty-fourth Birthday

The Sunlight and the Fog

The sunlight and the fog on early morning dew
tumble over barricades of yellow daffodils
and the words of robins pronouncing their language
of endless joy.
I've awakened there with you.

I've crossed the barriers like a blind man
with your hand in mine,
a gentle nudging out of the cave,
out of the mist of time into the searing light.

With you I have taken on the wisdom of old men
chewing on thin slices and drinking deeply in the night
with shaking hands so that tides of coffee
spill on old shirts grown gray and ragged.
And my song from never-tiring lips
is of a life born in the sound of a single chirp
of a distant chirping bird.

It is a sense of daffodils, a belief in deep yellow,
of a timeless freshness in the timeless morn.
I see your face.
The gate is open,
and I walk toward your magical throne
without footsteps.

For Imaging on her 67th birthday.

Tiger Lilies

You were young like a budded tiger lily
and I was forty.
I asked, "Whatever shall we do
when I am fifty and you're but forty?"
You said,
"For now it's all right for you and me,
so let's just wait and see."

Then I was fifty and you were forty
(and still quite nifty).
Worried, of course, I asked again,
"Whatever shall we do
when I am sixty and you're but fifty?"
You said. "Oh, dear,
it's that question once more.
Please, don't be such a lovely bore.
Don't you know beyond all knowing
that for now we're where we ought to be?
So shouldn't we just wait and see?"

Then one day I was sixty and you a fifty pixie.
Ever worried, I begged to know:
"When I am seventy and you but sixty,
then whatever shall we do?
I'll be so old, and, yes, I'm told
that living with the aged
is not the promised years of gold."
And you, still young and beautiful
like a tiger lily in full bloom, answered
with soft eyes and loving lips,
and a swish of those still youthful hips,
"Oh, please, can't we just wait and see—
just this once, for me?"

In a flash I was seventy and you at sixty,
now unable to hide your total beauty
like a bouquet of glorious tiger lilies in full bloom,
and I, deeply worried
with evidence of time stamped on my face
(and other places) I cried,
"Whatever shall we do when I am eighty
and you're but seventy?
Can you bear to be with skin over storage
of too much porridge,
a creaky fat old man
who only thinks he can?"
"Oh, my," you sighed.
"Oh, my, oh, me,
why should we dine
on such pie in the sky?
Please, just this once let's wait and see."

Then this day on the 9th of May,
your birthday dear darling—
the years had slipped passed
like a whisper in the wind.
I was eighty and you, still a wondrous,
ageless, lively seventy.
Yet fretting I whispered,
"Whatever shall we do
when I am ninety and you but eighty?
Whatever can we think
of such a time when I'll be in the drink?
And you, as usual,
still beautiful and in the pink?"
You looked at me like one couldn't learn.
"Who knows?" you said with no concern.
"Let's wait and see.

For once, let's just be silly sillies.
We may catch a glimpse of one another
waving to each other as lilies
in a field of tiger lilies."

On Imaging's 70th

We Washed the Mud Away

Come with me, I said.
And you followed me
behind the dark green shadows.

We could not find our way,
not through the shadows,
not through their verdant depths.

Then we walked into the sun
and laughed
like children playing in the mud.

And we washed the mud away.
Which is not to say
we ever stopped loving.

To Imaging on her 73rd

Facing the Ax-man

With wounded eyes I see that brave old tree,
scraggly barked, its trunk marked and scarred
by storm and drought of an injudicious century,
its head held high where noisy crows
scold in summer's heat and winter's cold
and larks with softer throats
sing with love-drenched notes
of sweet, delirious beat.

I see how its roots push out the pavement
to hold against wild and reckless winds
and sudden falling floods,
unrelenting, stubborn roots
spread like the thousand fingers
of a titan with a hundred hands
to vainly stand against the brutal ax-man
and his unforgiven, deadly plan.

Then old and scarred I asked,
"How do we survive the ax-man, dear tree,
we, our roots deep in the soil
and our old, stiffened limbs waving
at a patient, staring sky?"

In reply I heard strange tree-words
from the limb tops whispering,
"Listen with the heart."
And I listened with old ears
down into the silent deep
where perfect truth and wonder sleep.
And the dreaded purple fear departed.
For what I heard from heart and tree
were vital sounds resounding
from the soul of Earth,

from the bud of being,
sounds that have vibrated
across the landscape of my life,
through your loving words to me.

To Imaging on her 74th birthday, Montecito

Bound to the Great Inclusion

In the morning you are the gift.
The high choir keeps time to your breath.
There the cords of connection
hold you like a singing spider web
attached to half past eternity.

We are joined by fog and wing
by the nesting of the tiny titmouse
and the resting of trembling seas.
Your ears hear the heartbeat of the trees
ringing their silent songs of serenity.

Bound to the great inclusion,
fettered to elephant and ant,
to rock and jungles in the night,
your fingers float across my heart
like radiant rays of morning light.

For Imaging on her 76th Birthday

The Abounding Stream

No trudging through distant, sweating ranges,
to celebrate the power of our being,
over up-go, down-go trails
through ominous peaks that hold hands
and wait.
And wait.

And we?

No words of love without words of forgiveness,
no melodies of togetherness
without the gift of separateness,
no dark memories without worn scars of regret
that give new growth to fecund souls and stronger hands,
no promises that have not been kept,
in this abounding stream of life.

No.

No brooding genius of far-flung sciences,
can calculate, nor at last surmise
without surprise
that unfathomable sum
that represents our past together,
and our lives to come.

To Imaging 7-23-2015

I Was with You When

I was with you when
we were boys—
mere shaving boys.
We thought we were men
beyond the marching masses,
beyond the sheep who sleep in soft silken
corporate pajamas, covering
sold-out lackeys' asses.

I was with you when
we were adolescents.
Already we were half the years
of those "old men," we called them,
who'd begun to fear the distant calling.
We found time for soul searching.
And laughed because we couldn't find the soul.
I called it "scouring of the gut,"
a time for feeling, like a spider tangled in its own web,
like a snail who dies trying to cross a small crack
in the summer's scorching pavement
to the saving grasses.

I was with you when
we'd matured into men,
finally.
We'd stumbled past our prime
but thought ourselves hanging
at the edge of the sweet sublime.
We'd learned how to transform the self
into the other.
We called it *"reversing roles,"*
and thereby we became our loving fathers
or our merciless mothers,
or the other way around,

or any who otherwise
had locked our lives in the pitiless pen
of pain, rejection or despise
when we thought they should have loved us,
and we discovered to our surprise
we were not so loveable.

We searched our past like scattered puzzle parts,
believing that when they were fitted
they'd reflect a portrait
of who we were—
who we'd never seen
(and who we were afraid to see).

I was with you when
we played such games
fomented from the heart,
games of magic metamorphosis.
We helped each other
discover the elusive other,
and by that dangerous dance
we discovered ourselves.
We became children again.
Children,
a sacred time when the wisdom of the species
is most abundant
and guarded by the fragile armor of their innocence.

I was with you when
we discovered the hiding self—
that came rolling out
like passing summer thunder.
We sought the golden grail,
the intimate, timid, beauty of the self
that denied the self
like one cannot believe in miracles.

And we shared ourselves
with lawyers for the people,
we, the confessed fearful,
we, the admitted often lost,
we, the sometimes speechless—
we taught those caring few
who trudge in hopeless places,
in courts and prisons where those in power
disgrace the damned, and hate the innocent,
where people's lawyers,
bearing their weary, wounded selves,
are despised by the dollar jugglers,
the sold out lackeys of our corporate masters.
We embraced the heroes of the profession—
those who, with little hope for just compensation
fight on,
and on
for the rights of the lost and the poor,
who fight not for their wealth,
not for the fecund funds of power and luxury
but for the helpless,
the forgotten,
the hated
and the damned—
for the powerless people.

"Be real!" we cried to the lawyers.
"Be open. Be vulnerable.
Acknowledge your fear,
for fear is the truth.
Jurors are like we.
They, too, are afraid."
And a magical joinder occurred
when we stood
open, soul-naked before them
and the universal truth of man-and-womankind
was born, like the innocent babe

wet and crying at the threshold
of justice.

We preached:
"All power is vested
in the open, unsealed self
whether lost or frightened,
in whatever simple, truthful ways
its purest feelings will reveal."
We were right.
We touched the lives of multitudes.
We made our gifts—
"the way" by which
to discover
the luminous light of self.
We preached, *it all begins with you.*
Thereby we gave ourselves the key
to unlock long locked doors—
of our adversaries, of the judges and the jurors—
all bearing their own weighty, searing burdens
in these savage, yet uncivilized wars called trials.

I was with you when
you grew old too soon.
You'd made a careless choice of genes,
and nursed your beloved pipe.
The lungs found no song
to sing to the burning of corpuscles
and the clogging of the works
where lurks the smile of life and death.

I was with you when
you once proclaimed, as if from on high:
(yes, I thought you spoke from there)
"We cannot enjoy a fervent, no-holds-barred commitment
to being alive,
without accepting the reality of dying."

Then you said,
> *"I refuse to waste a moment*
> worrying about my impending death.
> I'm going to spend whatever time I've been given
> experiencing the gift of life."

You faced death without a whimper.
I promised to make you live.
I sent you to the celebrated medics to be healed.
They claimed they'd tried enough and gave up—
just gave up.
(I wondered if on the verge of drowning
they would just give up
and float peacefully to the bottom).
And they sent you home to die.
And you died—
just up and died
as if it were nothing more
than another day for living.

I was not with you when
you died.
I regret that
down to my last cell.
I grieved a grief that promised
to digest my heart.
At long last, time has beaten back
the ceaseless retching of my loss.
I do not cry for you,
but for *my* loss.
But the scars have not abandoned
their demand for my relentless attention.

I was with you when your ashes fluttered by.
I came to speak to you.
I know you heard me.
You always did.

You always do.
There were, of course, those disbelievers
who shout their inharmonious noises of doubt,
but who will never know,
not having once reversed roles
with the living or the dead
who keep on living.

Sometimes you speak through my lips
and I hear you, and I see you,
actually,
that boyish grin
as if you were smiling at yourself.
Those who doubt would rout the spirits out
and claim
that lemonade is the meaning of life.
And I understand:
you are speaking through their lips as well.
You have always been a hard one to silence.
And I'm glad—so glad to still have you
just hanging around
as you always did,
and as you always will.

     5-27-15
     Remembering John C. Johnson

On Becoming a Tulip

If I were a tulip
or a lover with two lips
especially if I were red
unwilted, and fresh as red daisies,
my bud puckered for the kiss,
I'd be prepared to begin my proclamation
of my love for you.

So there I stood, digested
in the petals,
consumed in the breath
of red tulips.
And when I looked up, I saw you,
and my words fled like tiny fluttering birds
who flew into your arms.

On Valentine's Day, for Imaging, 2017

THE WYOMING I KNOW

The old shoe tells nothing.
Nothing.
It lies silent as a cursed rock,
twisted as crooked dreams,
and wise in its eternal knowing,
like Jesus singing in the desert.

Cloth in a Deserted Cabin Window

It could have been a bridal veil
or a curtain.
One can't be certain.
It's a touchable memory
blowing in the wind.
I have touched memories too,
embraced them,
and gone on.

Homesteaders

These cabins held a breed,
men who were afraid,
but more afraid to be afraid,
to face their women
who stood brave.

These cabins, these sodded roofs
sheltered in a foot of snow.
The floors of dirt
unhurt by dripping boots
and muddy skirts.

I knew the people—
with hard, broken hands
that could be tender,
set-jawed people
who dared the cold,
and shivered in the night
against the threat of freeze,
but thawed and laughed
in morning light,
and shook off the fright
like waking children.

Business at North Fork

(a true story)

The red-tailed hawk lay spread-eagle in the dust
at the front door steps of Lundy Thayer's house.
Its blood had dried, its eyes as big and red as rusty dimes,
and with a first look and quick turning away
what was the color of dried blood
and the hue of feathers was hard to say.

The red-tailed hawk had company.
Three feet to the south lay the smiling, severed head
of last year's Herford calf (lately of the freezer)
staring back at Lundy Thayer
with flat green eyes.

"Ya see my old tom cat in the tree over there?"
asked Lundy Thayer.
"Where?"
"That black thing hanging there is my old tom.
That hawk grabbed him by his hair,
and kilt him dead as hell with one big swoop.
But he couldn't make it over the trees,
so he just dropped old Tom. And there he hangs.
Good place fer a cat ta die,"
Lundy Thayer surmised with wizened eyes.

The old tom was looped over a willow branch
about fifteen feet off the ground,
tail and head together
like a swan diver frozen with a belly cramp.

Well, it just seemed right to me.
I mean, it all came out fair.
Lundy was the winner.
He lost his cat to catch the mouse

but he was a damn good shot
and got the red-tail from the front door steps
with his twelve gauge.
And the night before
he'd had calf's liver for his supper.

May 20, 1971

Mormon Pioneers

The desperate nameless staggered
onto the prairies without horse
or truck, with groundless hope
and ribs that spoke
of empty plates
and battered yokes.

They pulled their carts like beasts,
stumbling through the pages of history
against the ceaseless trickery
of the Sorcerer's beckoning hand
under menacing sky and boundless land.

Had we flown back
to those tracks of bones
and mud of blood,
had we
amassed
our tears across lost generations,
through waves of heat
and conflagrations
of wind and sleet,
none could repeat
the plague of hurt
of those who writhed
and prayed
under roofs of sod
and died on floors of dirt.

Sun and Ice

In floods of ice, immortal winters sing their songs
across the prairies, perishing in storms of ice.
And then the silence,
the hollow, frigid silence,
as soundless as frozen frogs.

Nothing stirs, no mice scurrying,
the chirping gophers chilled to icy cell,
gay crickets dead as old twigs.
No bug or lice or snake, all stunned,
all stricken
in earth's refrigerated hell.

The land's too cold to shudder,
the windmills muted
in frozen grease of wheel
and rudder, too cold to spin,
the blades too stiff to cry,
the frozen sky, too cold to breathe
the birds of feathered wing too cold to fly.
And I, stiff as dead daisies,
stood in that hypothermic land
stood numb as dead trees
fried dry in bitter freeze.

Then the shrouded sun
came prowling through tall gloom
like old men whispering from the tomb
and laughed its cold and bloodless laugh.
And I? I stood too deeply frozen
in that endless empty room
too stiff and chilled to half suppose

that April's alpine buttercups
could once again rise free
from their frozen womb
to dance
on their annual yellow springtime spree.

Shoshoni, the Forgotten Town

This was a rough and raunchy town
on a Saturday night.
The ranchers came hooting in
looking for women
looking for sin,
the sheepherders, too,
randy as goats.

When the bus stopped
at the Blue Goose Café
during the day,
the girls waited the tables,
laid down the coffee
and fresh donuts,
and at night
laid themselves down.

No prejudice,
no hate,
all men equal
if they had the price
of "a short time"—
ten dollars to the banker,
five to the preacher.
"Next Sunday when they pass the plate
put the other five in for us,
and say a prayer—
just a short one, please
so when we step up to the gate
the Old Boy there will say,
'You did some good for lonely men, who
in their way
were men as hurt and hard as you.'"

Next door they served T-bones
as thick as bridge timbers
smothered in grease and French fries.
And the bartender
rendered double shots
with beer chasers to the women
and the women chasers.

Then the bus stopped stopping—
breezed on by,
and the coyotes were murdered
by coyote killers in Piper Cubs,
clubbed with buckshot
from the sky—
not a coyote left in a hundred miles.
No herders longer needed
to tend the flocks.
The ranchers were foreclosed by bankers,
and the preachers left
to pass their plates
at easier estates
and higher castes.
At last the town became a mocking memory
of wild, and wicked times now past.

The girls, unemployed,
and without unemployment compensation,
sought other fertile spaces,
so all that now remains
of its wild, uncultured graces
are those nostalgic traces
of naked laughter and bone dry hearts
in those empty, God forsaken places
called Shoshoni.

The Wyoming I Know

The Wyoming I know
in the long silent snow
and the short singing spring
is of the forgotten,
scared with weathered scars
of pitiless pain,
the thirsty prairie sod joined in begging
for early saving rain.

The people I know wore
hard, open faces with weighty eyes
and hopes as high as the cloudless sky.
They called themselves "settlers"
and hung to a few parched acres
and a cow or two with rattling ribs.

The ranchers, rich in land and poor in pity
ran them over with their hungry herds,
and with words of unconstrained disdain—
called them "squatters,"
those miserable scum who marred the land
with shacks and kids and took the water.

The people I know
were poor as ticks on the dead.
They yearned for place,
ripped up the sage,
and without song or verse
or times tender and gentle
they cursed adversity,
soaked the angry earth with sweat,
piled up hostile rocks for a homesteader's deed
to a hundred-sixty belligerent acres.
Then, as if satisfied,

they lay down
and quietly died.

The children—I saw them barefooted and wild,
laughing, chasing the cotton-tailed rabbits
and shunning the rattling snakes.
The children fishing,
the trout happy to oblige a child's dangling worm,
the children without shoes, calluses their soles,
and their souls clear as the creek.
But the children died from merciless killers—
of vile, peaking fevers,
the mothers too wounded to weep,
the fathers too weary to cry.
Then with hard, broken hands
they dug the graves
and buried their children,
one after the other—
Donna Mae, Peggy Marie,
Eva Darleen and Aloma Ann—
their graves marked
with small wooden crosses
bore their unbearable losses.
Then they thanked dear God
for taking them home
and silently prayed
to be saved.

The Wyoming I know
was of the foolish and brave
with bulging dreams and sunken bellies—
dreaming from beneath sod roofs,
their blistered feet on dirt floors,
dreaming without proof
that dreams could be touched
with broken fingers,
or grasped with bleeding hands
in such a raw and naked land.

The Wyoming I know was a place
where people were free to die,
but who struggled to survive
the slow, thirsty torture of drought,
their prayers for rain
answered with the invasion of scalding wind.
And fear and pain are met with muscled smiles,
and the grit of broken teeth.

Some owned a couple horses,
an old wagon, and a broken plow,
and all had a mortgage at the bank.
The bankers waited like hungry crows
to foreclose.
"Those sod-busters go broke
as fast as they come prancing into the state,"
a banker said.
"Then they claim we oughta give 'em
another chance,
another season.
The grasshoppers came.
That was the reason
the oats were eaten, and their horses
too weak to work, fell in their traces.
But there's no grasshopper clauses
in our mortgages," smiled the banker
without mercy or shame.

The bankers threw them out,
the children,
the weary mothers
who bathed once a week in the creek
and rose from their beds in the dark,
drove miles to church
after the chores were done,
after the old cow was milked,
the cream for butter separated,
the wobbly calf fed,

and the chickens served up yesterday's
skim milk, clabbered in the sun.

The bankers threw them out,
along with their worthless tin plates,
their empty kerosene lantern,
their splintered kitchen table, their broken chairs
their Holy Bible and Sears Roebuck catalogue,
that one old chest of drawers
with one suit of clothes
the husband would be buried in.

The Wyoming I know
was of hard times
and good times,
the people free as the long reaching sky.
Some days the people could see
for eighty miles or more.
The people could see their own bleak souls,
the people free as the long reaching sky.

Then the son who survived,
the one they said God had saved,
grew like the quaking aspens grow,
fast, and bending in the storms
he survived, and in gentle summer days
quaked as the aspens quakes,
laughed at hurt, laughed at the noisy loneliness,
and loved in short and breathless times.
And in the long days and into short nights
he and his woman busted up the sod
like his parents had.

This is the Wyoming I know.
Like the scorching sun,
there shines a solemn purity.
Some say they lived a foolish truth,

like the white sago lily bursting
through its bud
to the reckless promises of spring.

Then another deranged spring returned
with winter's rage in sweet relenting,
and the silvery pussy willows
exploded with willow-joy
like fuzzy boys showing off.
And of an early morning the meadowlark
shouted its missiles across the sage,
fighting its wars with yellow song,
and we sang with it.

We trembled in the thunderstorms
and laughed, we, safe behind the door.
Some days were as blue as bottles,
without a cloud, the cheerless shrouds
of lurking death and silent desperation,
dull and dreary,
having fled the golden morning light.

I have seen the distant mountains,
and the endless prairies.
I have watched my soul go bouncing
across the land like the playful jack rabbit,
without care, without fear
of the lurking coyote in its lair.

This is the wild Wyoming that I know,
where I grow young,
and as the years have passed
and the gray invades, younger still
until I have retreated as a child.

This Wyoming that I know
is a place ignored by the fancy

with their high cast chins
and low hung sensibilities,
whose power is like a noisy storm,
passing in the night with little rain—
this place, to me my hallowed home,
where I abandon the senseless race,
surrender my prized insanity,
and revive my lost humanity.

Driving the Herd to Slaughter

It's over.
String 'em out and run 'em through
this old cow town one last time.
They tread, heads down, to the slaughter house,
as we.

It's over—
the long days in sweeping mountain meadows
filled with alpine clover
and the song of forest thrushes
where a clear stream rushes,
tumbling by the blinking calf.

It's over.
The get of cow and man
shipped to the cities,
both to be devoured
by a savage nation,
without regrets,
gorged into gluttonous guts
that undulate
to the felonious noise of rap,
that shakes with the shakers
to the Wall Street minuets
against silhouettes
of high-rise glass and soulless steel.

It's over.
The old cows slaughtered
for McDonald's burgers,
their bawling calves,
and the sons of cowboys
consumed as veal
and as snake-oil money men

in this strange and noxious land
of smoke and calamitous clanging noise.
There, men have lost the feel
of the wide open spaces,
and women cry for their babies
of the mind,
traded in the market
for an equal stand with men.

The women, the men, the unborn and the dying,
all are lost in the frenzied pace,
all lost in their brawling in the bloodless war,
for the corporate glob was born dead
and those who are its warriors
have also died inside their paper dollar hides,
with the laughter of the dead
on their purple lips,
without thought of what comes after
when it's over.

It's over.
This is the last roundup.
We have abandoned the long prairies
and the endless, loping mountains.
We have abdicated this blessed realm
once the private land of antelope and prairie dogs
and those strange, mostly wild, intractable cowboys
whose home was on the range,
and who lived in the saddle—
all have surrendered
to a new horde of interlopers
who chop up the land
into mournful pieces
for the dead investment bankers
and the dead Wall Street takers
who hanker to become
real cowboys on twenty acres.
It's over.

Shelter

Ah, a roof
of boards or sod,
of shingles,
or tin that pops and jingles
in the wind,
a roof
by any hand
against blazing days
and freezing nights
that can withstand
floods of ice
and storms of sand
will suffice.

The People Are the Landscape

The people are the landscape.
The moon without people is no landscape.
Mars without the mar of men,
the scars of men
in strife across the land
is no landscape.

The people are the landscape.
The land, its trees
the moss clinging green,
without the settler's broken plow
in desperate dust,
without rotted posts,
and small potted flower gardens
hidden against boots and steel clad hoofs
is no landscape.

The people are the landscape.
The endless prairies
without ruts in mud,
(furrows on the forehead of the earth),
the swaying playing grasses,
the barren, distant hills
high in stark singing rocks,
without the song of prairie larks,
luscious, lyrical in the ears of people
are no landscape.

The people are the eyes
of mourning mountains
that without the eyes of people
stand blind,
stand silent,

stand frozen,
stiff and pitiable
without tears or eyes,
to fly in white delight
and bright surprise.

The people are the landscape,
their sweat, the flowing rivers,
their puddled sweat, the lakes,
their voices the distant thunder
that scorch the ears of people
and the tender ears of first hatch sparrows,
of curious gophers,
of scurrying prairie mice,
and of one small boy
who beat the gully-washer
to the front porch.

The people are the landscape,
the woman on the road grader
plowing out the last of winter's snow,
the wild crying Shoshoni dancing,
their days not yet done,
the shepherd by his wagon
lost in a landscape of bleating,
wool-clad faces furrowed in the sun—
their faces are the landscape,
hard, with no pretensions in the morning.

Death of the Pronghorn Fawn

The Laughing Lady Up in the Sky
thought it marvelously creative
to design the American Pronghorn
as a stand alone species—
one unrelated to goat or African antelope
or even sheep
and who, on three legs
can outrun California Chrome
at the Belmont's mile and a half,
then yawn, and take a sleep.

And, along with other jokes,
the said lady gifted the pronghorn fawn
with early speed—I mean early speed—
before a bird can fly or a cricket croaks,
within days the newborn pronghorn
can run 'long side the fastest member of the herd.

But man outsmarted the Laughing Lady
and built fences to mark his territory,
whereas the coyote lifts its leg,
and the meadowlark warbles its rivals
out of its private prairie province.

However, the Laughing Lady Up in the Sky
got so randy romping around up there
with Old What's His Name
she forgot to endow the pronghorn
with a fundamental skill—
to jump.
        To jump?
        Yes.
The pronghorn can run
as fast as a Model A Ford

in high gear with the wind at its rump.
And on a clear day
the pronghorn can see a flea hop
at the top of the horizon
twenty miles away.
But the poor pronghorn cannot jump.

The Laughing Lady
made all other four-leggers jumpers.
A rhinoceros and even an elephant
can jump over a small hump,
and what about a kangaroo
with two legs too few?
A hog, a dog and a frog, yes, all can jump.
But can the poor pronghorn jump?
No,
not even over a shrunken prairie stump.

So hot and haughty man
is out there thumping his chest
shooting off his mouth and his guns,
marking his territory
with fences,
with maps of fences,
boundaries recorded
in the county clerks' offices—
fences without sense
that chew up enough innocent trees for posts
to build a four lane bridge across the Atlantic,
along with enough barbed wire
to encompass the world and back
three hundred twenty-two times,
exactly.

Man's fence lines impose malevolent powers,
namely, to incite killing.
If one man steps over another man's fence line

he will actually kill his own species
along with old women with crooked, crippled fingers
and wide-eyed blinking children
licking orange and purple lollipops,
and all other living things
as permitted under the Constitution
to preserve his private property.

When a coyote yearns for a tender dinner
of antelope fawn, he and his fluffy-tailed,
sharp-toothed compadres
will corner the fawn against a barbed wire fence
of five barbed strands, the bottom stand
too close to the ground
for even a skinny fawn to slip under.

Goodbye sweet fawn.
(Good name for a song).
Bye, bye.
And the coyotes will begin their meal
to the bleat of the fawn's piteous squeal
and eat its liver while the fawn's high cry
melds with the song of the lark
throbbing across a stark, cerulean, Wyoming sky.

If I could advise the Laughing Lady
and Old What's His Name
(or whomever she's hanging with at the moment)
I'd tell them to build a world
without fences. None. Nada. Nowhere.
Teach man how to pee his borders
or warble with the birds.
But the Laughing Lady never asked me.

June 2012

Tracks of Man

The horse collars
have outlived the horse.
The windmill in the desert
whirls on
beyond
the time
of hard hands
that raised it
one day
to pump hard water
for a thirsty herd,
the builder now decayed
in some forgotten grave,
his sweat and blood absorbed
in this perpetual orb.

Old country stores
in desperate towns
built by men,
suffered by women,
their forgotten names
on stones,
unknown,
unremembered,
scars on the land,
the shacks crumbling
their last remaining tracks.

When the Neighbors Left

When the neighbors left,
their old pickup truck
was stuffed chuck full
with three kids,
the jumble of their junk
that wouldn't bring
ten dollars
at a rummage sale,
a half-collie,
half-coyote pup,
white with brown spots—
and one wooden pen
of their best laying hens.

They planned to come back
in the spring
for the bed springs left on the porch,
bring the kids for one last fling,
and the pup almost grown,
but that was forty years or so
ago.

Old Shoe

The old shoe tells nothing.
Nothing.
It lies silent as a cursed rock,
twisted as crooked dreams,
and wise in its eternal knowing,
like Jesus singing in the desert.

The old shoe,
not of fancy foreign hide,
but tough and sturdy
as it struggled over heavy mountain miles
and trudged deep into deadly, lost arroyos
until its knotted strings were rotted,
its immortal soul
like Jesus dancing in the desert.

And after the burial
beneath the long dead tree
that waved a leafless, maddened finger
at heaven,
they tossed the old shoe on the floorboards
over by the east window,
forgotten,
like Jesus preaching in the desert.

5-17-15

About Gerry Spence

Born, reared, and educated in Wyoming, Gerry Spence is recognized nationwide for his legacy of powerful courtroom victories and as the founder of the nationally acclaimed Trial Lawyers College, which established a revolutionary method for training lawyers to work for social justice. He has spent his career, both as an attorney and as a teacher of attorneys, striving on behalf of ordinary citizens.

He has received numerous awards including an Honorary Doctor of Laws degree from the University of Wyoming, and in 2009 was inducted into the American Trial Lawyers Hall of Fame. Gerry Spence is the author of eighteen other books, including the best-selling *How to Argue and Win Every Time* and the widely-acclaimed novel, *Half-Moon and Empty Stars*. He lives in Jackson Hole, Wyoming, with his wife of forty years, Imaging. They have six children and thirteen grandchildren.

The collected poems in this volume, written over a span of fifty years, offer insightful windows into the life and passions of Gerry Spence, the man who would become one of the great American lawyers of our time.

Enjoy other Sastrugi Press Titles

Blood, Water, Wind, and Stone, **edited by Lori Howe**
Wyoming is the least-populated state in America, and it is filled with long, silent stretches of prairie, mountains that see snowfall every month of the year, and a red desert. The pieces in this anthology relate what it is like to live at the intersection between human lives and needs, and the environment of the high plains and the mountains—to mingle our ephemeral blood with the shaping forces of water, wind, and stone.

Antarctic Tears **by Aaron Linsdau**
What would make someone give up a career to ski alone across Antarctica to the South Pole? This inspirational true story will make readers both cheer and cry. Fighting skin-freezing temperatures, disease, and emotional breakdown, Aaron Linsdau exposes the harsh realities of the world's largest wilderness. Discover what drives someone to the brink of destruction to pursue a dream.

Cloudshade **by Lori Howe**
In every season, life on America's high plains is at once harsh and beautiful, liberating and isolated, welcoming and unforgiving. The poetry of *Cloudshade* takes us through those seasons. Extraordinarily relatable, *Cloudshade* swings wide a door to life in the West, both for lovers of poetry and for those who don't normally read poems. Available in print and audiobook formats.

Voices at Twilight **by Lori Howe**
Voices at Twilight is a collection of poems, historical essays, and photographs that offer the reader a visual tour of twelve past and present Wyoming ghost towns. Contained within are travel directions, GPS coordinates, and tips for intrepid readers who wish to experience these unique towns and town sites for themselves.

Visit Sastrugi Press on the web at www.sastrugipress.com to purchase the above titles in bulk. They are also available from your local bookstore or online retailers in print, e-book, or audiobook form.

Thank you for choosing Sastrugi Press.
"Turn the Page Loose"